REVISED AND UPDATED

AMAZING JOURNEYS

Up a Rainforest Tree

Carole Telford and Rod Theodorou

Heinemann Library
Chicago, Illinois

© 1998, 2006 Heinemann Library
a division of Reed Elsevier Inc.
Chicago, Illinois

Customer Service 888-454-2279
Visit our website at www.heinemannraintree.com

Designed by Victoria Bevan, Michelle Lisseter, and Bridge Creative Services
Illustrations by Stephen Lings and Jane Pickering at Linden Artists
Printed and bound in China by WKT

10 09 08 07 06
10 9 8 7 6 5 4 3 2 1

New edition ISBN: 1 4034 8793 6 (hardback)
                   1 4034 8800 2 (paperback)

The Library of Congress cataloged the first edition as follows:
Theodorou, Rod
  Up a rainforest tree / Rod Theodorou and Carole Telford.
     p. cm. -- (Amazing journeys)
  Includes bibliographical references and index.
  Summary: Discusses the plants, animals, environment and conservation of the Amazon rainforest.
  ISBN 1-57572-156-2
  1. Rain forest animals -- Amazon River Region -- Juvenile literature. 2. Rain forest ecology -- Nests -- Amazon River Region -- Juvenile literature. [1. Rain forest ecology -- Amazon River Region. 2. Ecology -- Amazon River Region.]
  I. Telford, Carole, 1961- . II. Title. III. Series: Theodorou, Rod. Amazing journeys.
  QL112.48 1997
  577.34--dc21
     97-13743
     CIP
     AC

Acknowledgments
The publishers would like to thank the following for permission to reproduce photographs:
Ardea London Ltd. (John S. Dunning) p. 11 (top), (Nick Gordon) p. 14; Bruce Coleman Limited (Jorg and Petra Wegner) p. 13 (bottom), (Staffan Widstrand) p. 6, (Dr. Eckhart Pott) p. 25 (top), (Gunter Ziesler) p. 17 (bottom); FLPA (Roger Wilmshurst) p. 21 (top); NHPA (Elizabeth MacAndrew) p. 18, (Haroldo Pala) p. 11 (bottom, Jany Sauvanet) pp. 13 (top), 23 (bottom), 27, (Martin Wendler) p. 26; Oxford Scientific Films (Michael Fogden) pp. 17 (top), 19 (top), 21 (bottom), 24, (Paul Franklin) p. 12, Richard Packwood) p. 15 (bottom), (P. and W. Ward) p. 15 (top). Opposite: Oxford Scientific Films.

Cover photograph of a black-handed spider monkey reproduced with permission of FLPA/ Foto Natura/ Flip De Nooyer.

Every effort has been made to contact copyright holders of any material reproduced in this book. Any omissions will be rectified in subsequent printings if notice is given to the publishers.

The paper used to print this book comes from sustainable resources.

Contents

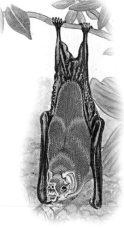

Some words in the text are bold, **like this**. You can find out what these words mean by looking in the Glossary.

Introduction

You are about to go on an amazing journey. You are going to travel to one of the most special places in the world: the Amazon **rainforest**. This is home to one in five of all **species** of plants and half of all species of birds in the world! You will cross the dark, gloomy floor of the forest and then travel up the mighty trunk of a rainforest tree. You will discover how each part of the tree is home to different kinds of plants and animals. Each animal has its own special way to move, feed, and **breed** in this amazing world of trees.

Thousands of species of trees, plants, and animals live in this rich **habitat**, which is as hot and **humid** as a greenhouse.

Tropical rainforests grow in areas of the world where it is hot, but where there is also a lot of rain. The Amazon rainforest is the largest rainforest in the world. It covers an area about two-thirds the size of the United States. It is also one of the wettest areas in the world. Two-thirds of Earth's freshwater can be found here! There are no **seasons**. It is always very hot and very wet.

The Amazon rainforest grows around the mighty Amazon River in South America.

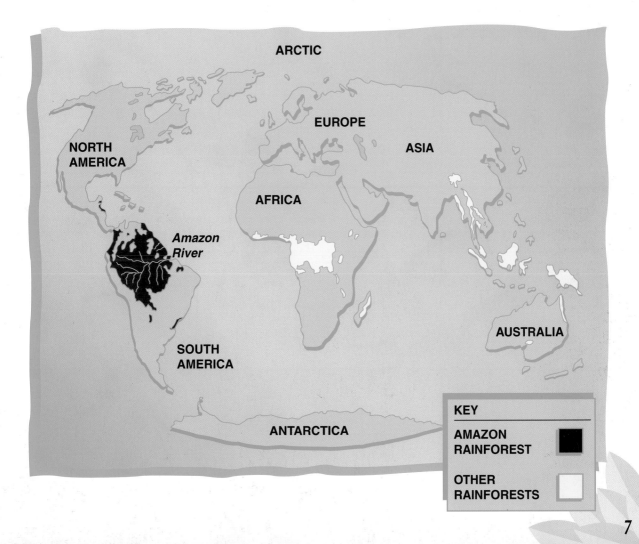

ARCTIC

EUROPE

ASIA

NORTH
AMERICA

AFRICA

*Amazon
River*

SOUTH
AMERICA

AUSTRALIA

ANTARCTICA

KEY	
AMAZON RAINFOREST	■
OTHER RAINFORESTS	□

Journey Map

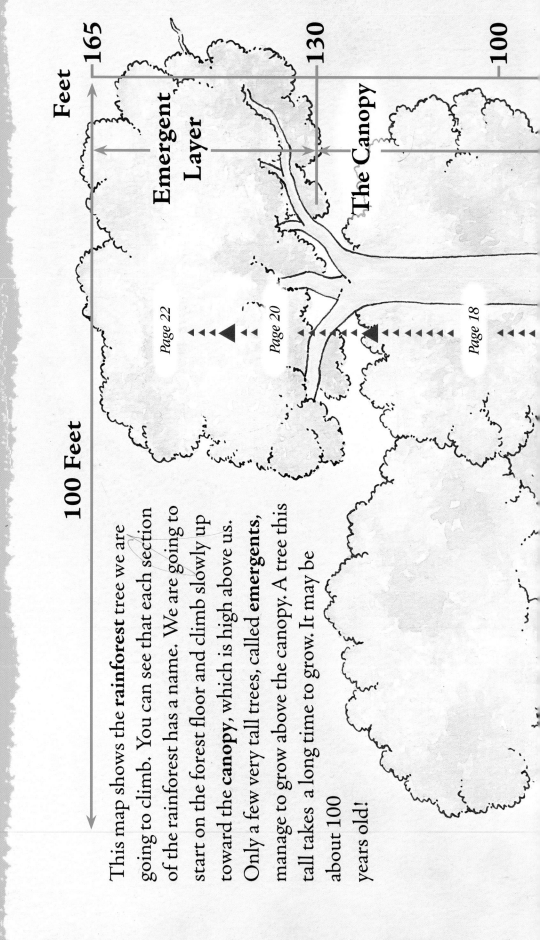

Feet

165

130

100

Emergent Layer

The Canopy

Page 22

Page 20

Page 18

100 Feet

This map shows the **rainforest** tree we are going to climb. You can see that each section of the rainforest has a name. We are going to start on the forest floor and climb slowly up toward the **canopy**, which is high above us. Only a few very tall trees, called **emergents**, manage to grow above the canopy. A tree this tall takes a long time to grow. It may be about 100 years old!

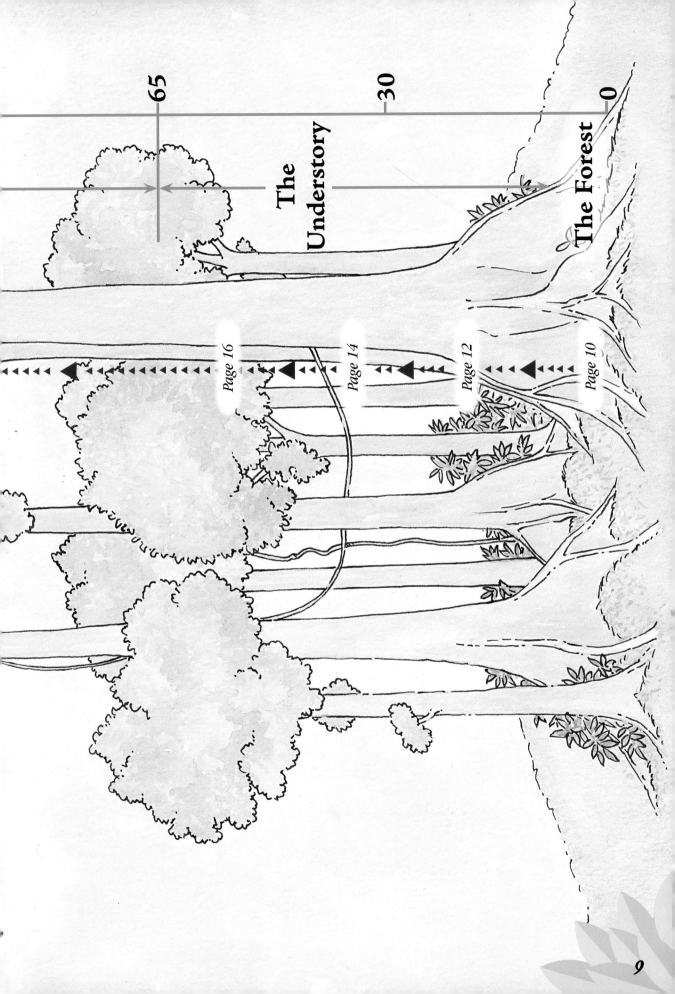

The Understory

The Forest

65

30

0

On the Forest Floor

We are walking through the **rainforest**. The air is full of the calls of birds and the buzz of insects. The air is **humid**, like in a hot, steamy shower. Even though it is daytime, it is quite dark. High above us, the thick **canopy** of leaves blocks out nearly all the sunlight. It is too dark for grass to grow. Instead, the ground under our feet is thick with twigs and dead leaves that have fallen from above. Many types of **fungi** grow here, helping to rot the **leaf litter**. The rotting leaves release **nutrients** that trees and plants take up into their roots to help them grow.

Fungi and rotting leaf litter provide food for thousands of tiny creatures such as beetles, ants, and wood lice.

rhinoceros beetle

crab spider

millipede

fungi

seedling

centipede

leaf-cutter ants

army ants

Antbird

This small forest bird has a special way of feeding. Army ants travel across the forest floor in rows, attacking insects and small animals. The antbird flies just ahead of the row and snaps up insects as they try to escape from the hungry ants.

Six-banded armadillo

The armadillo uses its strong claws to make a burrow to live in or to dig for tasty worms and insects. Although it is covered in strong, bony plates, it can curl up in a ball if attacked.

Rhinoceros beetle

These beetles are huge—as long as an adult's hand! Rhinoceros beetles are sometimes called Hercules beetles. The male uses his amazing horns to **wrestle** another male, trying to throw it over onto its back.

The Buttress Roots

As we look around in the gloom, we see **shrubs**, small trees, and larger tree trunks. Some trees have been able to grow much taller than the others. They have become giants of the forest, stretching their leaves up to the sunlit **canopy**. If we stand next to one of these trees, we feel tiny. Not only is it tall, but it also has huge roots. These special **buttress** roots anchor the tree into the **shallow** soil of the forest floor.

Some buttress roots grow up to 16 feet (5 meters) tall.

Cock-of-the-rock

This small, brightly colored bird eats insects and fruit. The cock-of-the-rock lives near the forest floor, where it dances and **displays** to other birds.

Coati

The coati has a striped coat that acts as **camouflage**. It uses its long snout to search out grubs and insects. It can also climb to hunt for birds and lizards.

Jaguar

The jaguar is the biggest cat in the **rainforest**. It lives alone and is an excellent climber and swimmer. It hunts fish, small animals such as mice, and large animals such as capybaras and coatis. With its spotted coat, it can blend into the shadows and creep up on its **prey**, such as this tapir.

The Understory

Now, we are climbing. The understory is the dark, gloomy area below the tree **canopy**. Because of the thick ceiling of trees, hardly any wind can blow down here. It is very still and **humid**. We are surrounded by ferns, palms, vines, and creepers, all dripping with **moisture**. They can live here because they do not need much light. Among the shadows and splashes of color, we spot lizards scurrying around, searching for food. A spotted ocelot climbs slowly up a creeper, looking for **roosting** birds.

Young **saplings** grow up toward the light in the gloomy understory.

Lianas

Lianas are climbing plants, called vines, that grow up other plants and trees. Many animals use these vines as ropes or bridges to travel around the forest.

Tarantulas

These huge spiders can grow as large as 10 inches (26 cm) across. They use their huge, poisonous fangs to catch other spiders, insects, frogs, and small lizards. Tarantulas are also called bird-eating spiders, but they only hunt small roosting birds or chicks.

Hoatzin

This strange bird nests in trees beside rivers in the **rainforest**. Baby hoatzins have claws on their wings to help them hold onto the nest and twigs. Hoatzins eat leaves that rot in their stomachs, giving off a disgusting, strong smell.

The Tree at Night

We decide to set up camp for the night in a fork in the tree. As the light fades, the **rainforest** comes alive with the sounds of **nocturnal** creatures. In the darkness, it is hard to see what is making the noise. The air vibrates with the sound of buzzing cicadas, grasshoppers, and croaking frogs. When we hear one frog croaking, we sometimes hear another answering back. A large moth flutters by. We see the shadowy shape of a bat swoop past to catch it.

insect-eating bat

silky anteater

termite nest

ocelot

fruit bats

nectar-sipping bat

16

Silky anteater

The silky anteater gets its name from its fine, soft coat. It lives all its life among the trees and vines, using its sharp claws and **prehensile** tail to climb. It hunts at night, feeding on ants and termites with its long, thin, sticky tongue.

Margay

This small cat, about 30 inches (80 cm) long, is related to the ocelot. It is a great climber and can leap with ease from branch to branch. Its creamy coat with black spots makes it hard to see as it hunts for birds and small animals.

Fruit bats

Fruit bats are sometimes called flying foxes. They feed on fruit, **nectar**, and **pollen**. Sometimes this pollen gets stuck on their fur and is carried to other flowers. This helps new plants to grow. During the day, they hang from branches as they sleep.

Toward the Light

It has been a long night. As day breaks in the forest, we begin our climb farther up toward the **canopy**. **Nocturnal** animals are hurrying to find a safe place to spend the daylight hours. Dawn brings a new chorus of birdsong. A large, grasshopper-like insect called a katydid freezes in front of us. In an instant, it looks exactly like a dead leaf. **Camouflage** is important in the **rainforest**. It protects animals from their enemies and helps them surprise their **prey**. We have to look carefully to spot snakes that look like vines and insects that look like leaves.

In the daylight hours, color and shape become very important for plants and animals.

Poison arrow frog

This frog does not use camouflage. Its colors are bright and easy to see. They are a warning sign to any **predator**. This frog has a poison in its skin that can kill even large predators such as snakes and monkeys.

Emerald boa

The emerald boa lives among the trees, where it uses its color as camouflage. It can grow up to 6.5 feet (2 meters) in length. It hunts parrots and monkeys, which it squeezes to death in its strong **coils**.

Praying mantis

This mantis is the same color as the leaves where it hides. It keeps completely still until another insect comes close. Then, it uses its fast and powerful front legs to grab its prey.

The Crowded Canopy

Now, we are into the **canopy**. It is less gloomy here and not as **humid**. It is hard to climb because the leaves and branches are so close together. All around we can hear birds and monkeys calling out. We can see many different types of monkeys using the vines to climb around us. Beautiful flowers grow here, and the trees are rich with fruit. Parrots and butterflies flash their dazzling colors.

More animals live in the canopy than anywhere else in the rainforest.

toucan

three-toed sloth

parrot

macaw

tamandua

woolly monkey

white-faced capuchin

green whip snake

Morpho butterfly

This large butterfly can measure up to 4 inches (10 cm) across its wings. It feeds on the **nectar** in flowers. The male morpho butterflies are the most brightly colored. Their color attracts a mate. They have special **scales** on their wings that catch the light and shine.

Three-toed sloth

This strange animal always moves very slowly. It hangs from branches all its life with powerful claws like hooks. Its fur is so damp and dirty that green **moss** and **algae** grow there. This helps to hide the sloth from its enemies.

Toucan

Many types of toucans live in the **rainforest**. Their long beaks and tongues can reach fruit growing on branches that are too thin to **perch** on. Sometimes they also eat lizards.

The Emergent Layer

At last, we reach sunlight! The **emergent** layer is made up of the tallest, oldest trees in the forest. The blazing hot Sun beats down on the tops of smaller trees around us, drying their leaves. It is far less **humid** here. There is even a gentle breeze. Here, it is much easier to spot brightly colored hummingbirds searching for flowers and fruits to feed on. We can also hear the loud whooping calls of howler monkeys.

The rainforest is home to 250 varieties of mammals and 1,800 **species** of birds.

fruit bat

spider monkey

Amazon parrot

blue-headed parrot

bromeliad

iguana

mouse opossum

Howler monkey

These are the largest and loudest monkeys in the **rainforest**. They have a special bone in their throat that acts like a trumpet when they call out. Their calls can be heard for miles, usually at dawn and dusk.

Hummingbird

By flapping their wings very fast, hummingbirds can hover and even fly backwards. They fly quickly from flower to flower among the branches, feeding off **nectar** with their long bills.

Gliding tree frog

The gliding tree frog climbs up tall trees and then jumps. Its webbed hands and feet act like parachutes, helping it glide to other trees over 40 feet (12 meters) away.

At the Treetop

Now, we are at the very top of our **rainforest** tree. We are just above the **canopy** on a platform of leaves swaying in the wind. The Sun is beating down fiercely. Insects fill the air, chased by **agile** birds. Around us in the canopy, we can see flashes of movement and color. Sharp-eyed eagles can also see them, and are ready to swoop down to snatch a monkey or parrot for a meal.

The view from the very top of the rainforest tree is spectacular!

Scarlet macaw

The rainforest is home to many different types of parrots. The scarlet macaw is one of the largest. Like most parrots, it can fly or climb through the branches and uses its strong beak to crack open nuts and fruit.

Spider monkey

This large monkey is too big to be hunted by eagles. With its long, thin legs and tail, it looks like a spider crawling through the branches. By drinking **nectar** from flowers, spider monkeys help the **pollination** of the forest.

Harpy eagle

The harpy eagle is the largest and most powerful bird in the rainforest. It is a fast and skilled **predator**. It can fly at speeds of up to 50 mph (80 km/h) through the branches to snatch monkeys or sloths in its strong **talons**.

Conservation and the Future

At the end of our journey, we enjoy one of the most wonderful views in the world—a view across the **rainforest** as it stretches in every direction, like a huge green carpet. However, we also see smoke in the distance, curling up between the trees. People are destroying the rainforest. Rainforests are being cut down for timber, fuel, or to make room for cattle to feed. Every second, an area of the Amazon rainforest the size of a football field is destroyed! This is a disaster for our planet.

Rainforests are the richest places on Earth, but every day they are being destroyed.

26

Why do we need rainforests?

Rainforests have been called the lungs of Earth. This is because trees in the rainforest release a gas called oxygen, which we need to breathe. When lots of trees are cut down, there is less oxygen and more of a gas called carbon dioxide. Too much carbon dioxide could make Earth hotter and cause great damage.

Once a rainforest has been cut down, it will never grow again. Tree roots hold the valuable soil in place. Without them, the soil washes away. Farmers often use the land for their cattle. The cattle eat the remaining plant life, leaving nothing but dust.

You can help save the rainforests by joining organizations that are working to preserve them. Thousands of **species** of animals need the rainforests to survive. Without these amazing places, it will be the end of their journey forever.

Rainforest animals such as Humboldt's monkeys are already in danger of extinction.

Glossary

agile   can move quickly

algae   very small plants that live in water and damp places

breed   to make more young animals

buttress   to push against and prop up

camouflage   colors or shapes that make an animal hard to see

canopy   tallest layer of trees in the forest

coils   rings a snake can form with its body to squeeze the animal it catches

display   show off brightly colored feathers

emergent   tree that grows above the canopy, toward the light

fungi   soft, spongy plant, such as a mushroom

habitat   place in which an animal lives

humid   hot and steamy

leaf litter   rotting leaves and plants that lie on the forest floor

liana   twisting, climbing plant

moisture   tiny drops of water that make something feel damp

moss   type of tiny plant that grows in damp places

nectar   sweet liquid like honey that some plants make to attract birds, bats, and insects

nocturnal   animal that is active at night and that rests during the day

nutrient   substance taken in by plants and animals to help them grow

perch	sit or rest
pollen	tiny yellow grains produced by male parts of plants that help the female parts to make seeds
pollination	transfer of pollen from the male to female part of a flower, which makes seeds
predator	animal that hunts and kills other animals for food
prehensile	flexible tail that an animal can use to hold onto branches
prey	animal that is caught and eaten by another animal
rainforest	forest in a warm place with heavy rainfall
roosting	sleeping on a perch
sapling	young tree
scales	thin flakes that coat the wings of a butterfly
season	part of the year that has a certain kind of weather
shallow	thin layer
shrub	low, bushy plant
species	group of living things that are very similar
talon	sharp claw of a hunting bird
wrestle	to hold onto and try to throw down

Find Out More

Further reading

Green, Jen. *Rainforest: DK Revealed*. New York: Dorling Kindersley, 2004.

Lynch, Emma. *Rainforest Food Chains*. Chicago: Heinemann Library, 2005.

Senior, Kathryn. *Life in a Rain Forest*. New York: Scholastic, 2005.

Organizations

Kids Saving the Rainforest

Manuel Antonio, Costa Rica

www.kidssavingtherainforest.org

Rainforest Foundation

32 Broadway

Suite 1614

New York, N.Y. 10004

www.rainforestfoundation.org

Using the Internet

If you want to find out more about rainforests, you can go to one of the website addresses below. Otherwise, you can use a search engine, such as www.yahooligans.com or www.internet4kids.com, and type in a keyword such as "rainforest" or a related subject such as "scarlet macaw."

Websites

www.rainforestfoundation.org/1child

The Rainforest Foundation works for the preservation of the rainforests, and its website includes an area just for kids.

www.kidssavingtherainforest.org

The site for Kids Saving the Rainforest includes puzzles, games, and interesting facts about the rainforest.

Index